T0156845

WELCOME TO COLLEGE!

101

WAYS TO
ROCK YOUR
WORLD

FOR ON CAMPUS AND HIGHER EDUCATION SUCCESS

Other books by speaker and success strategist Dayna Steele:

On the Golf Course: 101 Ways to Rock Your World

101 Ways to Rock Your World: Everyday Activities for Success Every Day

Rock to the Top: What I Learned about Success from the World's Greatest Rock Stars

WELCOME TO COLLEGE!

101

WAYS TO
ROCK YOUR
WORLD

FOR ON CAMPUS AND HIGHER EDUCATION SUCCESS

"This book serves as a road map for the challenges ahead, as well as a compass for when you get lost; use it to learn as much outside of the classroom as you will inside."

– Erin Callihan, Senior Director Interactive Media & Global Communications, NYU New York | NYU Abu Dhabi

By DAYNA STEELE
and PAGE GROSSMAN

Illustrated By **Ryan Nitsch**
Foreword by CNN Political Contributor Paul Begala

WELCOME TO COLLEGE!
101 WAYS TO ROCK YOUR WORLD

Copyright: Daily Success LLC 2014
Illustrations copyright: Daily Success LLC 2014

iUniverse books may be ordered through booksellers or by contacting:

iUniverse
1663 Liberty Drive
Bloomington, IN 47403
www.iuniverse.com
1-800-Authors (1-800-288-4677)

Disclaimer: The tips in this book do not guarantee success in college, nor
do the authors guarantee you will succeed in college. The only person who
can make that happen is the reader. Period. Now get back to work.

ISBN: 978-1-4917-3630-2 (sc)
ISBN: 978-1-4917-3629-6 (e)

Library of Congress Control Number: 2014909767

Printed in the United States of America.

iUniverse rev. date: 06/27/2014

To Dack and Nick,
for your college funds.
Love, Mom
—Dayna

To my dad,
for teaching me how to soar.
—Page

I have never let my schooling interfere with my education.

—Mark Twain

Contents

Perplexity is the beginning of knowledge.

—Khalil Gibran

Foreword

We parents like to joke that we spend the first year teaching our kids how to walk and talk, and the next seventeen telling them to sit down and shut up. It's a constant process, raising a child. Every day there's a little nudge, a little praise, a little consolation.

And then there are the *moments*: first tooth, first word, first fender bender, first heartbreak. There are pageants and plays and proms; baseball, basketball, and biology labs. Those moments stand out, but the real work of parenting is day to day. Raising a child is like braces on teeth: things only move the right way through constant contact.

But what do we do when the braces come off? Teeth lack free will, so they pretty much stay put when you remove the braces. Kids, of course, are capable of all kinds of unpredictable movement. So when we release our kids into the world, when they have slipped the surly bonds of parenting and flown free—it can be terrifying. For them as well as for us.

That's why this book is so important. Dayna Steele has collected 101 sound and sensible suggestions for college success. This book is what a friend of mine calls mother wisdom—perhaps literally. Since I have known Dayna nearly all my life, I feel as if I can hear her mother, Fran, or my mother, Peggy, saying these things to us as kids in the seventies in Missouri City, Texas.

It's all just good common sense. But of course, among college students common sense is not too common. If the young person you buy this for throws it in a backpack and just leafs through it a few times, it will be more than worth it.

Let me be clear: I admire today's college students. I have taught at three universities, and I am endlessly impressed by the quality of this generation of young people. They are much smarter than my generation. More communitarian. They understand the seamless garment of destiny that binds us all—maybe because they're Internet babies. As digital natives, they are unable to even comprehend that on the day Bill Clinton became president, there were fifty sites on the World Wide Web—fifty. They have fewer prejudices, more idealism, and less fear than their parents, who were taught to duck and cover when the inevitable Soviet ICBMs arrived.

So I am actually confident in the generation that will soon run the world. Some are even calling them the next Greatest Generation. That is how I see them as a professor. But as a father, I know they're also a bunch of knuckleheads, careening into early adulthood without the sense God gave a goat. How on earth am I supposed to trust them to run their lives and direct their education when it seems like just five minutes ago that I was changing their diapers?

This book will be my bridge, my source of comfort, my security blanket. It will be my kids' owner's manual for college. As we send our kids off to spend the money we've saved since the day they were born, we'll spend a few more dollars on this book to protect our investment.

Pro tip: slip a twenty-dollar bill into this book, around page 75. Don't tell your kid. If he or she reads that far, there's a good chance he or she will be just fine. Might even call to thank you, which could open up a whole conversation about how things are going and which of these lessons he or she is applying.

Hook 'em Horns!

—Paul Begala
Washington, DC
March 26, 2014

About Paul Begala

Paul Begala is a CNN political commentator and diehard Texas Longhorn. As counselor to the president in the Clinton White House, he coordinated policy, politics, and communications. He is an affiliated professor of public policy at Georgetown and is the author of several books on political policy. Paul and Dayna are proud graduates of Dulles High School in Stafford, Texas.

Acknowledgments

Since this is a book for college students, I would like to thank my family alma mater, Texas A&M University, for three generations of education (Whoop! '24, '52, and would-have-been '80). Thanks to the US Air Force Academy for the education and training you instilled in Charlie the Wonder Husband. Thank you, Western State Colorado University, for educating Cris and introducing him to the most amazing bonus daughter, Elizabeth. Thank you to the University of Texas for accepting Dack. Thank you to Clear Horizons Early College High School for accepting Nick. And one more thanks to Texas A&M University, in advance, for accepting Nick in the fall of 2018 …

Thank you to the Bain family for producing and introducing me to my brilliant coauthor Page Grossman. She has been a pleasure to work with on this book, and I cannot wait to see where she goes and what she does in this big world.

It is impossible to write and publish a book without editors. I continue to enjoy my experience with all at iUniverse and appreciate all this self-publishing entity does from beginning to end each time I take this journey.

Thanks to Linda Lee and Susan Neuhalfen, good girl friends who always agree to edit my books time and time again for wine.

To longtime friend, the very brilliant Paul Begala, for the foreword for this book and his passion for politics, family, and the University of Texas.

To Mom and Dad for my love of learning. And to Charlie and my three sons who continue to educate me on the finer things in life, love, and science fiction.

Gig' em!

—Dayna Steele

I'd like to express my love and gratitude to my mom, Lisa Bain Grossman, and aunt, Julie Bain, for their unceasing willingness to edit my writing and patience in forming me to be the writer that I am today. I owe much of my success and ability as a writer to them.

Thank you to my coauthor Dayna for accepting me into her family of rock stars. I'm so honored to work with her and to have this opportunity to write for her. She is such an inspiration and a testament to the fact that I can do what I love and find success at the same time.

My dear friends also deserve my thanks. I don't consider myself the only expert on college success. Many of these tips came from brainstorming sessions and Skype dates with my friends who have graduated and gone on to become great successes. I'd like to specifically thank Nick Schlekewey, Brittany Ray, and Megan Marks. Thank you all for sharing your great tips, for always being there for me, and for just being awesome friends.

Without my education I would not be the person that I am today. I would like to thank my alma mater, the University of Oklahoma; and the Joe C. and Carole Kerr McClendon Honors College for providing a fantastic and well-rounded education. The people that I met on that campus are ones who have changed my life and will be my friends for the rest of my days. I'd like to say a special thank you to my professors: Julie M. Jones, PhD; John C. Schmeltzer; Susan H. Caldwell, PhD; Victor K. Youritzen; and Tom W. Boyd, PhD. I see the world and myself differently because of the lessons that they have taught me. I thank them for giving me the opportunity to seek success and to know what it is when I find it.

Boomer Sooner!

—Page Grossman

> *If this book is a gift, there is a place for you to write your own personal note on the next page.*

Dear College Student ...

To my son Dack,

This book is a high school graduation gift to you. If all goes as planned, you will be headed off to the University of Texas in a couple of months to start the next chapter in this adventure we call life.

As I wrote and put this book together, you were constantly on my mind. I could picture you in each and every tip. Some may work for you, some you may choose to ignore, and some you will wish you had heeded our advice better. Whatever you do, know you inspired it all and continue to inspire me every day.

Your dad has a PhD, and I made it through only a year and a half of college before I left to pursue my passion of radio. Whatever you decide to do, know we love you and support you (emotionally). Be the rock star and good man I know you were meant to be—at whatever it is that rocks your world. I have given you the tips, the tools, and the love.

Now it is up to you.

With love,
Mom aka Dayna Steele

Write a note to your favorite college student here:

_____

_____

_____

_____

_____

_____

_____

_____

_____

_____

_____

_____

_____

_____

In the Beginning

Early to bed and early to rise makes a man healthy, wealthy, and wise.

—Benjamin Franklin

1. Get up early and attack your day.

Just because your class starts at noon doesn't mean you should roll out of bed at 11:45 a.m. Get up; take some time to prepare for your day without being rushed— review homework, eat breakfast, start a daily routine, stretch, and so on.

2.   Take care of yourself.

You'll be surrounded by a lot more people in college, which increases the likelihood that you'll get sick. Also, most college students' schedules mean that they're getting less sleep, exercise, and healthy foods. This combination can weaken your immune system. And remember, the best way to prevent sickness is to wash your hands—often.

> *Months are different in college, especially freshman year. Too much happens. Every freshman month equals six regular months—they're like dog months.*
>
> —Rainbow Rowell, *Fangirl*

3. Watch when, what, and how much you eat.

Part of college is getting to eat whatever you want whenever you want for the first time in your life. There's always an overabundance of free pizza on college campuses. Figure out what your eating weaknesses are and find ways to combat them. If you need to snack while studying, find healthy snacks you like, such as carrots, nuts, or hummus. Plus, remember that soda and beer are full of empty calories. Beware the "Freshman 15"—those extra fifteen pounds really do sneak up on many students!

> *Almost one quarter of students gained a significant amount of weight during their first semester of college.*
>
> —Nutrition Journal

4. Brush your teeth.

There'll be long days and late nights in college. You often won't be able to brush your teeth after every meal. So, commit to brushing your teeth every night, no matter what comes up, right before you fall asleep. Remembering to brush your teeth is a lot more comfortable than a root canal for most people.

> *You don't have to brush all your teeth—*
> *just the ones you want to keep.*
>
> —Unknown

5. Dress for how you want to be treated.

The way you dress affects how people perceive you. If you come to class every day in pajama pants or workout clothes, your professor may not think you'd be suitable for an office environment and may give that coveted internship to someone else.

> *You can have anything you want in life if you dress for it.*
>
> —Edith Head

6. Learn to be patient.

The transition from high school to university is harder than you think. Even if you took AP or IB courses, some college classes will be very difficult. If you were top ten in your graduating class, some things in college will still be tough. You'll now be a big fish who plopped into a much bigger pond full of other big fish. Swim fast.

7. Be confident.

Confidence is sexy. Find skills that you excel at and concentrate on those to bring you confidence. Focus on your strengths. And the things that scare you? Just keep doing them until you build up confidence in those areas as well. Remember when you learned to ride a bike? Same thing.

> *Confidence is contagious. So is lack of confidence.*
>
> —Vince Lombardi

8. Be responsible—you're in charge now.

College is the first time most students live away from home. Now that you get to make all of your own decisions, think before you act, and imagine any consequences to your actions. Other people are counting on you now as well. It's important to fulfill your responsibilities, such as paying your bills on time, arriving promptly for appointments, and keeping up with your laundry.

> *If you take responsibility for yourself, you will develop a hunger to accomplish your dreams.*
>
> —Les Brown

9. Solve your own problems.

You're now an adult, so your mom should not call your English professor about the C you got on your paper. You must face it and solve it yourself. It's okay to ask for help and advice, especially if you don't know how to do something, but don't rely on others to fix things for you. Universities are full of resources. Use them.

> *Find a solution, or management will. And you probably won't like the one management comes up with.*
>
> —Charlie Justiz

10. Mind your social media habits.

Social media is a prevalent and important tool in relationships, business, and society. It can, however, become a time vampire and career-ruining device if you're not careful. While studying, turn off your notifications and focus; don't jump back and forth between homework and social media. Don't experience everything through the lens of your phone. And watch what you post—many employers look back at your posts before they decide to hire you or not. Just because you've deleted something doesn't mean it is gone for good.

> *I have a choice. I can either watch all the dailies. Or I can follow social media. I can't do both.*
>
> —Steven Spielberg

11. Protect yourself from crimes of opportunity.

Put a passcode on your phone and laptop. Don't leave your things unattended. Be aware of the people around you, keep your purse or wallet close, and don't step away from your laptop in the library. Be alert at all times. Don't walk alone at night.

> The most common passwords of 2013 were 123456, password, 12345678, QWERTY, and abc123.
>
> —SplashData

12. Make a budget and stick to it.

College is a great time to start thinking about your financial future. Every student is in a different financial situation. Some work, some have loans, and others have an allowance from their parents. Figure out how much you can spend per month; don't go over that and start saving some of it. Use a credit card only for emergencies. A good rule of thumb: if you don't have cash for those jeans or that video game, don't buy it.

> *I believe that we parents must encourage our children to become educated, so they can get into a good college we cannot afford.*
>
> —Dave Barry

13. Apply for scholarships.

Go for all the scholarships you can. Every extra bit of money that you can get to help pay for college makes a difference. There are scholarships for everything, even being left-handed. Start looking in the financial aid department and then in your major's department.

14. Prepare for the weather.

Many students attend a college that's far away from home, which might mean a completely different climate. Do a little research and find out if it rains a lot, if there's a harsh winter, or if you're going to have to endure broiling heat. Prepare yourself with the right clothes to be comfortable in that environment.

> *You can't get mad at weather because weather's not about you. Apply that lesson to most other aspects of life.*
>
> —Douglas Coupland

15. Create your best study environment.

During college, it's important to figure out how you work best. Some people need silence; some need music while they study. Learn how to combat fatigue and discouragement. Always remember, the human brain recalls information better when it is in the same frame of mind as when it learned that information.

> *Recipe for success: study while others are sleeping; work while others are loafing; prepare while others are playing; and dream while others are wishing.*
>
> —William Ward

16. Build a community.

Create a network around yourself by being kind to people, doing favors for them, and asking about their lives. Your college friends become your family away from home. Your new network could help you find an internship or a job in the future.

> *It takes a village.*
>
> —Unknown

17. Fight homesickness at the first signs.

Don't be afraid to talk about feeling homesick. It's normal for students living away from home for the first time. Try to stay on campus for at least the first three weeks. Start getting involved. As you build a community (see #16) on campus, it'll start to feel like home, and the homesickness will quickly go away.

I'd rather be homesick than home.

—Leo Vroman

18. Figure out what kind of learner you are.

You might be an aural, kinesthetic, or oral learner. It's important to find out how you learn best so that you can study properly and make the most of sitting in class listening to professors. Search online for *what kind of learner am I* and try any number of online quizzes and games to determine your learning style.

> *The only person who is educated is the one who has learned how to learn and change.*
>
> —Carl Rogers

19. You choose your major.

This is your life and your time to figure out what you want to do with it. If you choose your major based on what classes sound the most interesting, you'll be more likely to graduate, love your future job, and be successful. Don't choose your major based on how much money your job will make in the future, and don't let anyone else choose your major for you. It's okay not to know what you want to do when you first start. Take a few general classes, and then decide. And, if your parents are paying for your education, at least give them the courtesy of a discussion concerning your decisions.

> *Passion is energy. Feel the power that comes from focusing on what excites you.*
>
> —Oprah Winfrey

20. Have a backup plan.

Consider declaring a minor or a double major so that you'll always have a second option. This is especially important if you choose a major in the arts. Pair an arts or communications degree with a business, entrepreneurial, or marketing degree.

> *The true sign of intelligence is not knowledge but imagination.*
>
> —Albert Einstein

DORM
SWEET
DORM

21. Live in an on-campus dorm your freshman year.

The friends that you make on your hallway and floor will last you the rest of college, if not your life. You have an automatic, built-in community that will help you get involved in campus life. The dorms are usually centrally located, which makes it easy to get to class. Cafeterias are provided, which eases the burden of planning menus, shopping, cooking, and cleaning up. And it's a good experience in learning to compromise and work things out with others.

My roommate got a pet elephant. Then it got lost. It's in the apartment somewhere.

—Steven Wright

22. Do not live with your best friend.

It may seem like it would be tons of fun to live with your best friend, but most friendships don't survive that stressful environment. It's better to live with someone who you know shares similar living habits as you, and know that you can see your best friend as often (or not) as you want. Best friends make bad roommates.

23. Have the roommate talk.

Have a talk with your new roommate as soon as possible. Ask questions such as: When do you sleep and study? Do you like to have music or the TV on? Blinds closed? Who is going to take out the trash and clean the bathroom? How do you feel about loaning clothes? How late and how often will your "special friend" be with us? The sooner you understand how your roommate works and lives, the sooner you can compromise and create a happy living environment for all involved.

24. Compromise and forgive.

You won't always get your way in college, so learn to let go of the little things. They're not that important. And forgive people for being different from you. You have enough to worry about without adding that to your list.

> *I hate the fact that people think "compromise" is a dirty word.*
>
> —Barbara Bush

25. Smile at strangers.

Everyone feels lonely sometimes. Don't be afraid to smile and say hi to people you don't know or sit down at lunch with someone who is alone. Great friendships are often built on small gestures. Your small gesture might be the nicest thing that happens to that person all day.

> *Smile—it's free therapy.*
>
> —Douglas Horton

I try to prepare for everything beyond the extent of preparation.

—Taylor Swift

Prepare to
Succeed

26. Have a plan.

College can be intimidating. For the first time, students have more freedom and are starting to decide what they want to do with the rest of their lives. Before you start your sophomore year, it helps to formulate a two or three semester plan. Know what classes you want and need as you move forward. This will help you graduate on time. And remember, some classes are only offered once a year.

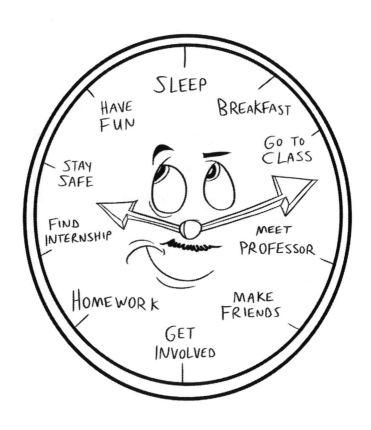

27. Set time limits.

Knowing how much time you have to complete a task helps keep you focused on just that task and motivates you to get it done in that amount of time—from how long you study to how long you plan to stay in college.

28. Don't over-schedule yourself.

You came to college to get an education. It's important to get involved in campus life, but make sure you leave time to start thinking about your career and to get a good education. If you overload your schedule, all your work and activities could suffer. When you're too busy, you won't be sleeping enough, and the quality of your work will decline.

> *The key is not to prioritize what's on your schedule, but to schedule your priorities.*
>
> —Stephen Covey

29. Get familiar with the campus before your first class.

You don't want to be the one who walks into class late on the first day because you didn't know where the classroom or the building was. Don't be that person.

> *You only have one chance to make a first impression.*
>
> —Unknown

30. Know the rules of the university.

College is different from high school; you'll be treated as an adult, and ignorance of the rules is not a defense. Most universities have very explicit written policies for the dorms, alcohol use, and academic integrity. It's important to find those policies, read them, and understand the risks and penalties.

> *Integrity has no need of rules.*
>
> —Albert Camus

31. Pack your backpack the night before.

You'll have more time to think about what you might need, and you'll be less likely to forget something. Toss in a snack to keep your brain functioning in case of a late night or unexpected meeting.

32. Organize your schedule.

There are always fun events on a college campus, but if you go to every one, your homework will never get done. College is a great time to learn how to balance work and play. Whether you use the calendar organizer on your phone or a paper planner, include every event and commitment—including the fun stuff, tests, and due dates. And always have that planner with you.

> *I have my whole life organized on an 11 x 17 tear-away weekly calendar!*
>
> —Brooke Burke

33. Learn more names.

Remember the names of your classmates, the cafeteria workers, and your professors. It's a skill that takes practice and concentration, but try to memorize people's names when they introduce themselves. This is especially important for people you see often, such as the cleaning lady in your dorm or the gym attendants. If you forget, just ask. Don't try to guess.

34. Stay informed.

Reading the news is a great way to start your day because you'll know what people are talking about and will have ready-to-go topics of conversation. Stay informed about local, national, and international events; being well-educated will help you make decisions now and in the future about everything you do. Set a breaking-news alert from a network or cable news organization on your phone or tablet.

If you want to be an entrepreneur, it's not a job, it's a lifestyle. It defines you. Forget about vacations, about going home at 6 pm—last thing at night you'll send emails, first thing in the morning you'll read emails and you'll wake up in the middle of the night. But it's hugely rewarding as you're fulfilling something for yourself.

—Niklas Zennstrom

35. Return emails and phone calls.

Make it a habit to check your email at least twice a day. Respond promptly. Don't promise to do it later. Do it now. Everyone hates having to wait for an answer. Many professors use email to contact students, give assignments, and sometimes to cancel class. Future employers may also communicate with you this way. Get in the habit now.

36. If you make a commitment, honor it.

What you do the night before a big event is your business. Maturity means being able to show up, look presentable, and function the next morning. Know your limits, drink early or drink only a little, but make sure you show up prepared and ready to go. And yes, attending class is a commitment.

Commitment is an act, not a word.

—Jean-Paul Sartre

37. Be file-saving smart.

"I didn't remember to save" isn't an excuse for not turning in work. Learn to save after every paragraph, every few minutes, or better, turn your auto-save on. Create a file-naming system so you can find what you save, such as *classname_assignment#2_draft*. Make sure to back up your work using a cloud service such as Google Docs or DropBox. When you do that, you can work on your project anywhere and anytime, even on your phone.

As I told the students every time I visited a campus, you are the director of your own movie, and if you aren't enjoying what you are doing, change it.

—Gary Johnson

38. Take advantage of campus resources.

Most schools offer abundant resources for students, and they are often free or discounted. A few examples include health services, writing and research assistance, office hours, advisors, counseling services, and much more. Use them!

39. Find out who the rock-star professors are.

A good professor can make any subject interesting. Before you choose your schedule, ask other students which professors they like best. There are many sites that catalog and rate professors. Often the professor is more important than the class. Even if a rock-star professor is not in your field of study, take a class from him or her if you can. Just being in the presence of excellence can be inspiring.

40. Get to know your instructors.

College is not like high school. Professors and students are both at the university to learn and to do research. Don't be afraid to talk to your professors. In fact, introduce yourself early in the semester. In time, they'll become mentors and friends, much more than just teachers. Take advantage of office hours and drop into the office just to chat. These are the times that professors are required to sit in their offices and be available to help students. How would you feel if nobody came to talk to you?

> *The shortest distance between two people is a story.*
>
> —Patti Digh

41. Find your own answers.

Never be afraid to ask a question, but always take some time to look for the answer yourself first, or at least some information, by researching it online. There are, indeed, stupid questions, and those are usually caused by laziness.

> *Judge a man by his questions rather than his answers.*
>
> —Voltaire

42. Read your syllabi.

It might be boring reading material, but the class syllabus usually contains pertinent information about the attendance policy, how the final grade will be decided, when tests are scheduled, reading assignments, and other important matters. Always check the syllabus before asking the professor a question about the class.

> *Follow instructions. This sounds easy enough. It isn't. For some people, it's the key to most of their academic problems.*
>
> —Gary North

43. Learn how to research.

Finding and sorting through large volumes of information are necessary skills for college, jobs, and life. You must learn how to be thorough and fast. Many college libraries offer free workshops on this subject.

> *Research is formalized curiosity. It is poking and prying with a purpose.*
>
> —Zora Neale Hurston

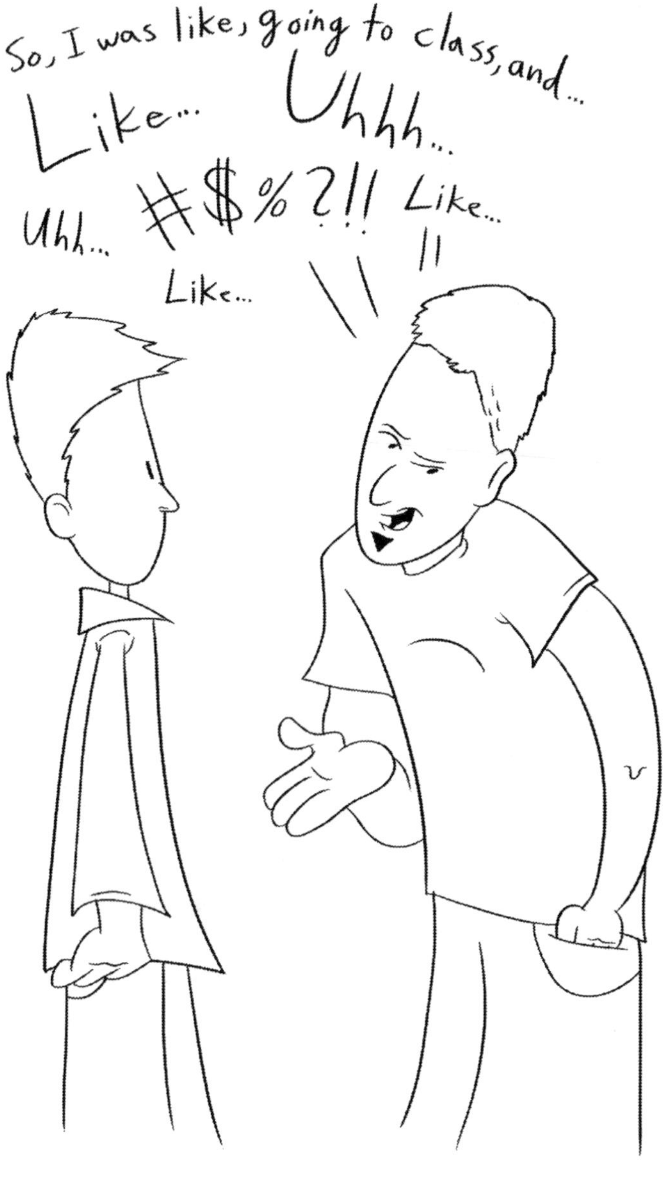
So, I was like, going to class, and...
Like... Uhhh...
Uhh... #$%?!! Like...
Like...

44. Aim to communicate well.

Being a good communicator and a clear, concise writer will benefit you in any field. Practice in your texts and emails. Track down the writing center at your university for more help. Listen to how you speak. Lose the uhs, likes, you knows, expletives, and whatevers. Lose those now. For good.

45. Think independently and discover who you are.

Take time in college to challenge the beliefs you were raised with and find out if they truly define you or if there's something that better fits your personality and the world around you. Also, don't let love cloud your judgment and force you to make a college decision that you otherwise would not. Don't let others make decisions for you—from what college to attend to what classes to take to how you believe. You'll change and mature over the next few years. Enjoy the adventure.

Knowledge is true opinion.

—Plato

46. Stick to your convictions.

Peer pressure isn't just in movies—it's an element of life that will follow you forever. If you don't want to do something, say no firmly and keep repeating it, or remove yourself from the situation. There's no need to be embarrassed by the things you believe in or by the things you don't want to do.

The resume focuses on you and the past. The cover letter focuses on the employer and the future. Tell the hiring professional what you can do to benefit the organization in the future.

—Joyce Lane Kennedy, *Cover Letters For Dummies*

47. Start a resume and keep it updated.

You never know when an internship or job opportunity will pop up. Go to the college resource center or check online for resume samples. Keep it updated with activities, classes, awards, charity projects, and additional relevant information. Be sure to save it in that filing system you created (see #37). Have someone proofread it carefully before you send it out.

48. Plan ahead for an internship.

If you're interested in getting an internship, it's important to start looking and applying early. Many summer internship applications are due in December and January. If you're looking for a summer job, start looking before spring break. Whether it's a job or an internship you want, start telling family, friends, and professors what it is you're looking for as soon as you decide.

*I'm not going to vacuum until Sears makes
one you can ride on.*

—Roseanne Barr

49. Keep your space tidy.

This is especially important if you must share your space with a roommate or if you choose to bring someone over to study or for a date. No one wants to walk into your room to study and find that everything is covered in dirty clothes and old food. There's no need for your room to be spotless at all times, but be respectful of guests and roommates. Clean sheets and a made bed are not bad ideas either. Just in case …

50. Minimize distractions.

When you're doing a job, focus. Give it your full attention; don't try to multitask. *Health Magazine* found that experts estimate switching between tasks can cause a 40 percent loss in productivity. This means putting your phone away or putting it on silent and closing other windows online while working on a paper or homework. Focus on one thing—the task at hand.

The classroom should be an entrance into the world, not an escape from it.

—John Clardi

In the Classroom

When you are in my classroom, you get everything from me. But you bloody well better give everything too.

—Tony Judt

51. Take general education classes during the summer or intersession.

Get some of the easy classes done in the summer, when you can take them in a more condensed time period. They'll be over faster and cost less if taken at a community college. This also frees your time in the semester to take more interesting classes, graduate on time, and possibly even relax during your senior year.

52. Consider online classes.

Taking a course online sounds wonderful: no lectures, flexible schedules, and easy tests. The hardest parts of online classes are self-motivation and discipline. Don't leave all of the assignments and tests until the end of the class. Make yourself a schedule and stick to it. If you can do that, you'll like the flexibility these classes give you.

53. Take a class outside
your major.

Try a completely new subject you know nothing about, maybe even something that scares you. Have you always wanted to learn Russian or wished you could paint like your artistic roommate? Take a discussion class and see what happens when you challenge your beliefs. College is the time to explore these things. You may discover a new passion or talent. Or at the very least, make new friends.

> *It is not the strongest of the species that survive, nor the most intelligent, but the one most responsive to change.*
>
> —Charles Darwin

54. Go to class.

There will be days when this is the hardest tip to follow. You stayed up too late or just don't want to sit through one more hour of your professor yammering on about a subject you never wanted to study in the first place. At the end of the semester, when you might need a recommendation letter or a little leeway on your grade, professors always remember who was in class and who wasn't. Surprisingly, some professors do take roll. Some even give bonus points to those in attendance. Work very hard to practice this tip. Every class.

> *It is harder to conceal ignorance than to acquire knowledge.*
>
> —Arnold H. Glasow

55. Leave technology at the door.

Laptops and tablets are useful devices for taking notes, but they're also the fastest way to find yourself not listening to the professor. Before entering a classroom, silence all devices and think about turning off your Internet connection. No Internet means no distractions.

A man who wants to lead the orchestra, must turn his back on the crowd.

—Max Lucado

56. Sit in the front of the classroom.

In a lecture hall of four hundred students, the professor will only remember your face and your name if he or she can actually see you. When you need help with homework or have a question about an assignment, the instructor will appreciate that you attend class regularly. Plus, if you sit in the back, you may find yourself distracted by all the computer screens of your classmates.

You have got to pay attention, you have got to study and you have to do your homework. You have to score higher than everybody else. Otherwise, there is always somebody there waiting to take your place.

—Daisy Fuentes

57. Pay attention in class.

Though some lectures may be boring, the professor is probably providing important information. Take notes in class and try to understand the lecture. If you spent the time getting to class, you may as well pay attention and learn something. Then, odds are you'll have to study less for the test later.

58. Handwrite notes.

If you're a slow writer and feel more comfortable typing, it's okay to take notes on your computer. But then go home and handwrite the important points from your digital notes. Consider this part of studying and reviewing material. Google *muscle memory*—writing something by hand is a form of memory creation.

59. Speak up in class.

State your opinion. Participating in class discussions helps the professor recognize who you are. It also teaches you how to be more articulate and how to state opinions without insulting others. Learning how to craft, dissect, and defend a verbal argument is a good life skill.

> *The most courageous act is still to think for yourself. Aloud.*
>
> —Coco Chanel

60. Learn to apply each lesson to the bigger picture.

Every lecture and class is like a piece of a puzzle. To see the whole picture, you need to put the pieces together. During the semester, remember to take each segment of teaching and figure out how it fits into the larger theme of the class, as well as your major or future profession.

> *I'd compare college tuition to paying for a personal trainer at an athletic club. We professors play the roles of trainers, giving people access to the equipment (books, labs, our expertise) and after that, it is our job to be demanding.*
>
> —Randy Pausch, *The Last Lecture*

61. Make at least one friend in every class.

If you miss class or get sick, you can ask this friend to take notes for you. You can do the same for him or her in return. You'll always have a study buddy.

62. Review previous tests to study for the next one.

Understand a professor's style of writing test questions by reviewing the tests you've already taken. Some professors keep old tests and will allow students to study those as well. You can also ask a friend who previously took the class or use test files saved by sororities, fraternities, and other groups. You'll be able to better predict and answer what the professor will ask next time, as well as know the correct answers to the questions when they reappear on midterms and finals.

College has given me the confidence to fail.

—Jarod Kintz, *This Book Has No Title*

63. Be a good borrower.

If you borrow something, such as class notes or a test (see #62), give it back in a timely manner and in good shape. That person did you a favor—now it's your job to return it. Don't make him or her hunt you down. Also, be careful who you let borrow things from you.

> *Worry is the interest paid by those who borrow trouble.*
>
> —George Washington

64. Don't procrastinate.

There are a thousand and one ways to avoid doing your work. The best way to get it done is to begin. If you can force yourself to sit down and start the work, you can finish the project. If you're writing a paper and you can't figure out a way to introduce your topic, start writing in the middle and work on the beginning later.

> *I'd be more frightened by not using whatever abilities I'd been given. I'd be even more frightened by procrastination and laziness.*
>
> —Denzel Washington

65. Do not cheat.

Depending upon the university that you attend, there will be different rules on how cheating is defined, but most universities are much more strict than high schools. Working on homework in a group can even be considered cheating. Make sure to read your university's cheating and academic integrity policy. If you can't find it, ask a professor; he or she will be impressed that you care. Just to be clear: *do not cheat, do not cheat, do not cheat.*

> *All good is hard. All evil is easy. Dying, losing, cheating and mediocrity are all easy. Stay away from easy.*
>
> —Scott Alexander

66. Do your homework.

Your job as a college student is to get an education, and a big part of that is doing homework and studying to learn the material. Don't procrastinate (see #64), and do your homework. It's part of the process in school and in real life. Do the work that must be done in order to succeed.

A college education should equip one to entertain three things: a friend, an idea, and oneself.

—Thomas Ehrlich

Keep
Learning

Educate thyself through reading.

—Ann Shannon

67. Study hard, but not all at once.

It's not beneficial to cram and stay up all night before your test. The information that you do manage to learn will slip right back out of your tired brain. An article published in January 2013 by the Association for Psychological Science called "Improving Students' Learning With Effective Learning Techniques" concludes that students who study in many short sessions over a long period of time and use various study techniques will learn the material much better than a student who studies the material all at once.

68. Seek out lectures and conferences.

Look at the calendar of events at your school. Universities attract some of the brightest minds in the world, and these experts come and share their knowledge on everything from Middle Eastern politics to new technologies. All you have to do to broaden your education is to sit and listen for an hour or two. Bonus: many of these events are free, and some even have free food.

> *There is much pleasure to be gained from useless knowledge.*
>
> —Bertrand Russell

69. Take a speed-reading class.

Being able to read and comprehend material quickly will enable you to get your work done faster and better. Being a good and speedy reader is a skill that will benefit you in all classes and for the rest of your life.

> *Today knowledge has power. It controls access to opportunity and advancement.*
>
> —Peter Drucker

70. Volunteer for a leadership role.

Even if it's a small role, you can learn a lot about yourself by leading other people. You may even find that you don't like the pressures of being in charge, but you'll never know if you don't try. There is little risk in trying an influential position in college. There's usually someone willing to step in and help you if you get in over your head.

71. Learn to make yourself marketable.

When you graduate, your goal is to find a job. You need to participate in events and social groups during college that clearly demonstrate your skills to potential employers. Start looking for these groups during the second semester of your freshman year so your resume will show that you're involved in groups that will give you valuable experience for your future job.

> *Opportunities don't happen, you create them.*
>
> —Chris Grosser

72. Accept criticism gracefully.

You can learn so much from your mistakes and from the advice of professors and mentors. Criticism can hurt, but the quicker you can accept it and improve your skills, the faster you'll gain knowledge and be a successful student.

> *To avoid criticism, do nothing, say nothing and be nothing.*
>
> —Elbert Hubbard

73. Learn from your mistakes.

Just as you should learn from criticism (see #72), you should also learn from every mistake in college. Whether it's blowing a test because you didn't read the question or study the material correctly or flunking an entire class—figure out what you did wrong and don't make the same mistake ever again.

> Tip # 19: Learn from the mistake if you do fail.
>
> —From the original *101 Ways to Rock Your World:*
> *Everyday Activities for Success Every Day*

74. Work during college.

If you can, use your freshman year to have fun and figure out college, then get a job. You'll become a better time manager, you'll build relationships with adults, you'll learn how an adult work environment functions, and you'll begin to create a network of professionals who may help you in the future. Get a job that actually requires you to work. Though it will be tempting to become a computer lab attendant and just study while "working," it will benefit you and your resume a lot more to have a job that will improve your professional skills. If possible, look for a job in your field. Once on the job, work hard to earn a great recommendation from your supervisor.

> *Experience: That most brutal of teachers.*
> *But you learn, my God do you learn.*
>
> —C. S. Lewis

75. Acquire experience during summer break.

Don't spend your summers sitting around. Instead, try to find an internship (see #48) or a job opportunity in your field of study. Or figure out what skills will be needed in the future workforce and acquire those. For example, as our relations with the Middle East increase, we need more people who can speak Arabic. Summers are your free time to do what you want; do something to continue your education. This might be a good time to try one of those online classes (see #52).

> *The only real security that a man can have in this world is a reserve of knowledge, experience and ability.*
>
> —Henry Ford

76. Beware of scammy internships.

Unpaid internships are quite common in certain industries, and if you can afford to do one, it can often lead to a great job. However, be wary of an internship that requires you to pay them. For any internship, do as much research as possible to be sure you'll get a lot of pertinent experience or at least college credit.

> Nick: You got us a job at Google?
>
> Billy: Well, not a job job. It's an interview for an internship that could lead to a job. Nick, this might be the last chance that we've got.
>
> —from *The Internship*

77. Make time for the fine arts.

University-produced dance, musical, opera, ballet, and art shows are the highest quality for the cheapest price you can find. Try one of each. Even if they are unfamiliar to you at first, you'll soon become comfortable and may find a new passion.

78. Make friends with an international student.

Getting to know someone from another country allows you to learn the intricacies of his or her culture and helps you to see your own in a different way. With an international friend you can discover another culture without ever leaving your room. He or she might even cook for you. Or better yet, let you visit his or her hometown in the future.

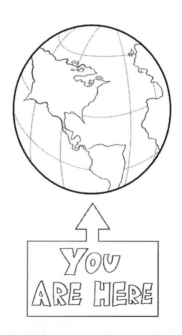

79. Travel or study abroad.

Actually living within a new culture changes your perspective and teaches you to see the world through someone else's eyes. You'll become better informed, more empathetic, and more adventuresome. Make every effort to grab any of these opportunities you can. Most universities offer some sort of study-abroad program as well as discounted summer learning opportunities. Pack your bags.

> He who does not travel does not know the value of men.
>
> —Moorish proverb

By going to the movies and because of other things, too, going to college, making a wide variety of friends, moving around traveling, I became a lot more open-minded than the heritage I was born into might have suggested.

—Roger Ebert

After Hours

Steele • Grossman

80. Step away from the phone.

It's important to live in the moment, to actually have a real-life conversation with someone, and to participate in what is happening. Don't just take photos and live on Facebook or see the world through Instagram. Join real life—it can be quite fascinating.

81. Make new friends.

College is a time to meet new people and build a new and larger community. Branch out. You'll grow more, learn more, and have more adventures. If you are attending a college with a lot of your high school friends, that's great but make new friends as well.

> *Friends and good manners will carry you where money can't.*
>
> —Margaret Walker

82. Go to "the Event."

Depending on where you go to school, the Event will be something different. At some schools, the Event is football. Even if you don't care anything about the actual game, it's important to go. There's nothing like the camaraderie you feel as you bond over a win or loss and dress up in school colors. Figure out what the Event is and go!

83. Say yes.

If someone asks you to go hear a local indie band or invites you for Passover Seder or to visit his or her hometown for Thanksgiving break, say yes. You'll create lots of new memories and bonds. You won't make many friends if you just sit in your dorm room.

> *I always defer to "yes."*
>
> —Guy Kawasaki

84. Be wary and aware of drugs.

There will be drugs in college. Marijuana, Adderall, and opiates (pain medication) are the most common drugs used by college students. Pot is still illegal in most states. It is also illegal (and dangerous) to take drugs prescribed for someone else. Buying, possessing, or selling Adderall, opiates, or other controlled substances is a crime and can result in serious consequences. Taking Adderall without a diagnosis of ADHD can also be viewed as cheating, by giving you an unfair advantage over others.

> *Slash sat me down at his house and said, "You've got to clean up your act." You know you've gone too far when Slash is saying you've got to get into rehab.*
>
> —Charlie Sheen

85. Don't leave your drink unattended.

The number-one safety rule for bars or parties is to always keep your hand on your drink. It's so easy for someone to spike or drug your drink when you turn away. It only takes a second of distraction. If you set your drink down, keep your hand over the open top. If you ever walk away from your drink, throw it out and get another. Your health and safety are more important than a few extra bucks.

> Every year more than 97,000 students between the ages of 18 and 24 are victims of alcohol-related sexual assault or date rape.
>
> —National Institute on Alcohol Abuse and Alcoholism

86. Stop sexual assault.

Memorize "no means no." When a potential partner says no, stop any further sexual activity. If she or he is passed out from drugs or alcohol, that is an automatic "no" and is considered rape by the law if taken any further. If you are the victim of sexual assault or "date rape," report it immediately to the authorities. Many campuses have hotlines and trained personnel who will come help you immediately. Or you may call the National Sexual Assault Hotline at 800-656-HOPE.

> *Perhaps most important, we need to keep saying to anyone out there who has ever been assaulted: you are not alone. We have your back. I've got your back.*
>
> —President Barack Obama
> *www.notalone.gov*

31 percent of college students met criteria for a diagnosis of alcohol abuse and 6 percent for a diagnosis of alcohol dependence in the past 12 months, according to questionnaire-based self-reports about their drinking.

—www.collegedrinkingprevention.gov

87. Know the signs of alcohol poisoning.

Passing out, blacking out, and memory loss are all indications of alcohol poisoning. If someone's showing these symptoms, you should get him or her to a hospital for treatment. If someone does pass out, roll that person onto his or her side. This can help prevent aspiration on vomit, choking, or even death. A trip to the hospital is better than a trip to the morgue. Many jurisdictions now have a "no arrest and no punishment" policy if you bring a drunk, underage friend to the hospital.

88. Drink water.

Make it a habit to drink water all day long. Water is good for your health and your weight. It's good for your skin. Also, hangovers are mostly a side effect of dehydration. Make sure to drink a big glass of water before going to sleep after a night of drinking. In fact, drink water before, during, and after your escapades. Drink water all the time. It's usually free and in abundance. It's one of the easiest things you can do to take care of yourself (see #2). Thirst is often mistaken for hunger.

WATER IS YOUR FRIEND

89. Use protection.

Sexually transmitted diseases are at an all-time high in college students. HPV is the most prevalent STD. You can also get it from oral sex, and it causes several types of cancer. Be safe and use condoms every time. It only takes one time to get pregnant or contract a life-threatening disease.

Wrap that rascal!

—Saying on a condom keychain
Houston rock radio station KLOL
used to give away to fans

Live as if you were to die tomorrow. Learn as if you were to live forever.

—Mahatma Gandhi

End of
the Day

It's fine to celebrate success, but it is more important to heed the lessons of failure.

—Bill Gates

90. Failure is an option.

There are plenty of ways to fail at college—surefire ways. Failure can be a particularly eye-opening way to learn what works and what doesn't work. But failing even one class can screw up your whole life plan if you're thinking about medical school or graduate school. People always advise you not to be afraid to try something new and fail at it. And college may be the time to make small mistakes and learn your limits (see #73). But remember, an epic failure could send you home.

91. Get home safely—every time.

If you have a late class or event, find someone to walk you home or call campus security. If you decide to drink, be sure that you have a way to get home safely. Make a plan ahead of time. It could be a taxi, a designated driver, or a walk with a buddy. If you don't have a safe way to get home, find a couch to curl up on and get some sleep. And, if you stop to get money for a ride, be aware of your surroundings when getting money from the ATM.

> *Be safe, sweetheart.*
>
> —Every mom in the universe

92. Give back to your community.

It's important to be involved in the university community as well as the city around you. Take time to find a way you can volunteer and give back. This will help others and make you feel good about yourself.

> *I'm a true believer of karma. You get what you give, whether it's bad or good.*
>
> —Sandra Bullock

93. Show appreciation.

If someone takes the time to do something nice for you, whether it's holding the door open or getting you the financial-aid paperwork you need, make sure to say thank you and always be polite. If someone goes out of his or her way to help you, send a handwritten thank-you note. It's a lost art in this digital age. It'll be appreciated. And you'll stand out and be memorable.

94. Keep in touch with family and friends.

College can be busy, fun, exciting, and stressful—all at the same time. There's always so much to do. Take time to call home (at least once a week) and make time to just hang out with friends—new ones or old ones. Relax and have some fun. Hanging out with friends relieves stress, makes you laugh, and helps create relationships that can last a lifetime. Calling home will probably make you feel good or, at least, make the people who raised you happy. Note: Parents would much rather hear your voice than get a text message.

> *The love of family and the admiration of friends is much more important than wealth and privilege.*
>
> —Charles Kuralt

95. Know going home will be weird.

With your new independence, it's strange to go home and live by the old family rules. You changed, but your home world did not. Have patience with your family and with your old friends when you return home for a visit or for the summer.

96. Remember you.

After you finish a task, give yourself a reward. This is especially helpful on those long nights of studying. Choose whatever will make you feel that you have accomplished something. It can be as simple as crossing that job off a checklist, eating some chocolate, or posting a status update. And remember to take some time for yourself. With everything going on in your life at college, it's important to do some activities that bring you joy and are solely for you.

> *What I am suggesting is hard work and it can be slow work, but the rewards are well worth it.*
>
> —Jesse Helms

97. Do not burn bridges.

Never, ever burn bridges with anyone. Even if you think your roommate or ex is the most awful person in the world, you may need a favor from him or her someday. Don't betray confidences, don't talk poorly of others, and let go of your animosity. What you put out there comes back to you. Be nice.

> *Burning bridges only makes it harder to get around and cover more ground.*
>
> —Unknown

98. Be flexible about your future job.

Your major does not necessarily determine your job for the rest of your life. Gain skills, experience, and relationships in college. Then be open to whatever comes your way. Many a successful person has started out in college in one direction and ended up in a completely unrelated career. Stay open-minded and curious about everything. You just may stumble upon your life's passion.

99. Review tomorrow's responsibilities before going to bed.

This will help you to be mentally prepared for the tasks you must accomplish the next day. It puts you one step ahead before you even wake up.

> *To be prepared is half the victory.*
>
> —Miguel de Cervantes

100. Study. Sleep. Repeat.

For every hour spent inside the classroom, you should spend two hours studying on your own. Going to lectures and labs is important, but it's only a small part of being a college student. As a student, your job is to learn the material that will make you a qualified employee, and possibly even an amazing success, in the future. To do that, you must study. Then get a good night's sleep, get up in the morning, and do it all over again.

> *You can't knock on opportunity's door and not be ready.*
>
> —Bruno Mars

Happiness doesn't depend on any external conditions; it is governed by our mental attitude.

—Dale Carnegie

101. Be happy.

Happiness is your choice. No other person can make that choice for you. If you are feeling unhappy, do something that makes you happy; smile, sing, take a walk, dance, do something that makes someone else happy, watch a funny movie—whatever it takes—it still comes down to the fact it's your decision whether or not to be happy.

You don't have to be a genius or a visionary or even a college graduate to be successful. You just need a framework and a dream.

—Michael Dell

Words from a Recent Grad

As a last few words of advice, I want to say, even if you think that college is not for you, take your SATs just in case. You may feel differently in a year after working a full-time job. As well, don't stress too much over which college you choose or are accepted to. All schools offer good educations. It's what you do while you're there and with the resources offered that makes you a success or not. You're the only one who can make the decision whether to put in the effort to be successful or not.

I'd also like to say, take all advice with a shot of skepticism. You're going to receive a lot of advice from parents, professors, other students, university function organizers, advisors, and this book. Judge for yourself if that advice works for you or not. You have to learn who you are, what you want to do, and how you will do it best. But keep an open mind and try some of it.

College is full of amazing experiences and really late nights of studying. You will experience some of the lowest lows of your life but also some of the highest highs. If you remember only one lesson from this book, remember, it's going to be all right. I promise, it will.

—Page Grossman

We can do anything we want. We're college students!

> —*National Lampoon's Animal House*

Checklist

1. Get up early and attack your day.

2. Take care of yourself.

3. Watch when, what, and how much you eat.

4. Brush your teeth.

5. Dress for how you want to be treated.

6. Learn to be patient.

7. Be confident.

8. Be responsible—you're in charge now.

9. Solve your own problems.

10. Mind your social media habits.

11. Protect yourself from crimes of opportunity.

12. Make a budget and stick to it.

13. Apply for scholarships.

14. Prepare for the weather.

15. Create your best study environment.

16. Build a community.

17. Fight homesickness at the first signs.

18. Figure out what kind of learner you are.

19. *You* choose your major.

20. Have a backup plan.

21. Live in an on-campus dorm your freshman year.

22. Do not live with your best friend.

23. Have the roommate talk.

24. Compromise and forgive.

25. Smile at strangers.

26. Have a plan.

27. Set time limits.

28. Don't over-schedule yourself.

29. Get familiar with the campus before your first class.

30. Know the rules of the university.

31. Pack your backpack the night before.

32. Organize your schedule.

33. Learn more names.

34. Stay informed.

35. Return emails and phone calls.

36. If you make a commitment, honor it.

37. Be file-saving smart.

38. Take advantage of campus resources.

39. Find out who the rock-star professors are.

40. Get to know your instructors.

41. Find your own answers.

42. Read your syllabi.

43. Learn how to research.

44. Aim to communicate well.

45. Think independently and discover who you are.

46. Stick to your convictions.

47. Start a resume and keep it updated.

48. Plan ahead for an internship.

49. Keep your space tidy.

50. Minimize distractions.

51. Take general education classes during the summer or intersession.

52. Consider online classes.

53. Take a class outside your major.

54. Go to class.

55. Leave technology at the door.

56. Sit in the front of the classroom.

57. Pay attention in class.

58. Handwrite notes.

59. Speak up in class.

60. Learn to apply each lesson to the bigger picture.

61. Make at least one friend in every class.

62. Review previous tests to study for the next one.

63. Be a good borrower.

64. Don't procrastinate.

65. *Do not cheat.*

66. Do your homework.

67. Study hard, but not all at once.

68. Seek out lectures and conferences.

69. Take a speed-reading class.

70. Volunteer for a leadership role.

71. Learn to make yourself marketable.

72. Accept criticism gracefully.

73. Learn from your mistakes.

74. Work during college.

75. Acquire experience during summer break.

76. Beware of scammy internships.

77. Make time for the fine arts.

78. Make friends with an international student.

79. Travel or study abroad.

80. Step away from the phone.

81. Make new friends.

82. Go to "the Event."

83. Say yes.

84. Be wary and aware of drugs.

85. Don't leave your drink unattended.

86. Stop sexual assault.

87. Know the signs of alcohol poisoning.

88. Drink water.

89. Use protection.

90. Failure is an option

91. Get home safely—every time.

92. Give back to your community.

93. Show appreciation.

94. Keep in touch with family and friends.

95. Know going home will be weird.

96. Remember *you*.

97. Do not burn bridges.

98. Be flexible about your future job.

99. Review tomorrow's responsibilities before going to bed.

100. Study. Sleep. Repeat.

101. Be happy.

For a printable copy of this checklist:
www.yourdailysuccesstip.com/101waystorock

But if you tell folks you're a college student, folks are so impressed. You can be a student in anything and not have to know anything. Just say toxicology or marine biokinesis, and the person you're talking to will change the subject to himself. If this doesn't work, mention the neural synapses of embryonic pigeons.

—Chuck Palahniuk

About the Authors

DAYNA STEELE YourDailySuccessTip.com CEO, is the author of the best-selling business book *Rock to the Top: What I Learned about Success from the World's Greatest Rock Stars,* as well as the creator of the *101 Ways to Rock Your World* book series. As a popular business speaker, she brings her unique background as a former top rock radio personality to captivated audiences with the Rock Star Principles of Success, based on her true brushes with the famous and infamous.

AOL calls Dayna "one of the foremost experts on career networking," and *Reader's Digest* magazine named Dayna one of the "35 People Who Inspire Us."

Dayna was named one of the "100 Most Important Radio Talk Show Hosts" by *Talkers* magazine, nominated as "Local Radio Personality of the Year" by *Billboard* magazine, and inducted into the Texas Radio Hall of Fame.

Dayna's daily success tip from YourDailySuccessTip. com is enjoyed by thousands of success-driven people around the world every day. She is a regular contributor to the *Huffington Post* and also founded Smart Girls Rock, giving laptops to high school students in need of personal technology. Dayna lives in Seabrook, Texas, with her husband, author Charles Justiz, and has three sons.

PAGE GROSSMAN

felt like a successful college student as she juggled academic success, sorority life, a part-time job, campus clubs, an occasional beer with friends, and a position on the university's academic integrity council. She was honored to receive an American Society of Magazine Editors summer internship, where she was thrilled to write for *Popular Science* magazine. She was also named the outstanding senior in the art history department. After four years, the University of Oklahoma confirmed her success in 2013 by granting her two bachelor degrees *magna cum laude*, in journalism and art history. Page accomplished all of this after losing her beloved father to a heart attack before her second semester in college.

Page lives near Fort Worth, Texas, and is currently working as a freelance journalist and social media specialist. She is also researching, writing, and curating for a small, private museum slated to open in Oklahoma in 2015. Her hobbies include reading, blues and salsa dancing, backpacking tourism, critiquing street art, and sharing Belgian sour ale with friends.

RYAN NITSCH is an illustrator, director, and animator. Currently finishing up his associate in art degree from Houston Community College, Ryan is weighing options to pursue a bachelor's degree in communications/media arts and animation. He is a member of Phi Theta Kappa Honor Society. While going to college, Ryan pursues a career in illustration and animation and is the founder of Find Your Niche Productions.

Contact Us

We hope you have enjoyed *Welcome to College! 101 Ways to Rock Your World*. Keep in touch and let us know how you are doing in college. If you have a question, feel free to ask us. And if you have an idea for another book in the *101 Ways to Rock Your World* book series, let us know. Here is our contact information:

Dayna Steele:
dayna@daynasteele.com
@daynasteele

Page Grossman:
page.grossman@gmail.com
@pagegrossman

Illustrator Ryan Nitsch:
www.ryannitsch.com

Speaking queries for Dayna and Page:
Wilene Dunn
713-518-4914
wilene@wcdenterprises.com

Quantity book purchase:
iUniverse
800-288-4677

Education is the most powerful weapon which you can use to change the world.

—Nelson Mandela

Final Thought

It is important that I am honest here at the end of this book. I did not finish college. I tripped over my passion in my freshman year when I auditioned for the student radio station on a dare. It is not something I had ever even remotely entertained doing in my life. In fact, I started college as a premed student, eventually switching my major to journalism and then theater. I basically changed my major and living arrangements every few months until my future passion presented itself in a way I would never have imagined. That said, most of the advice in this book is not just for college students. This is for anyone who would like to lead a happy, successful, and full life. Enjoy every minute of your college experience—and then find a way to do just that for the rest of your life. And never stop learning.

—Dayna Steele